chardonnay

chardonnay

a complete guide to the grape and the wines it produces

MITCHELL BEAZLEY

dave broom

chardonnay

by dave broom

First published in Great Britain in 2003
by Mitchell Beazley, an imprint of Octopus
Publishing Group Limited, 2–4 Heron Quays,
London E14 4JP.

A CIP catalogue record for this book is
available from the British Library.

ISBN: 1 84000 685 4

Commissioning editor   Hilary Lumsden
Executive art editor   Yasia Williams
Managing editor   Emma Rice
Design   Nicky Collings
Editor   Colette Campbell
Production   Alexis Coogan
Index   John Noble

Mitchell Beazley would like to thank the staff at
Oddbins in Camden High Street, London for their
help with the photography.

Typeset in RotisSansSerif

Printed and bound by
Toppan Printing Company in China

Picture acknowledgements
1, 2-3, 5 Octopus Publishing Group/Alan
Williams; 6 Octopus Publishing Group/Adrian
Lander; 13 Adrian Lander/Stok-Yard; 14-15
Scope/Jacques Guillard; 16-17 Adrian
Lander/Stok-Yard; 18-19, 20-21 VinVinoLife; 22-
23, 24 Octopus Publishing Group/Alan Williams;
27 Janet Price; 28-29 VinVinoLife; 30-31
Octopus Publishing Group/Alan Williams; 32-33
Corbis/Barry Lewis; 34-35 Janet Price; 37
Octopus Publishing Group/Alan Williams; 39
Root Stock/Hendrik Holler; 40-41 Janet Price; 42
Octopus Publishing Group/Alan Williams; 45
Root Stock/Hendrik Holler; 46-47 VinVinoLife;
48, 51, 52, 54, 55, 56, 58-59, 60-61, 62 Octopus
Publishing Group/Alan Williams.

contents

introduction

Ask anyone to name a white wine and the chances are
they'll say Chardonnay. It's not so much a grape variety
as a brand, and as such it has come in for some unfair
criticism recently. But there's much more to the mighty
Chardonnay than easy-drinking, oaky wines... it's the
most versatile grape in winemaking and the basis of
some serious world-class wines.

Chardonnay is a malleable grape and much of its character comes from the soil it is planted in, how much water it gets, how much sunlight it has been exposed to, and, finally, what the winemaker does with it. However, it does have certain physical characteristics that affect the way it tastes.

the chardonnay look

Skin

There is a relatively high level of pigment in the skin, which means that fully ripened grapes give a yellow-gold coloured wine. The skin also contains a surprisingly high number of aromatic compounds – smells of fruits and vanilla. But, the skin is quite thin and can suffer from rot problems if there is rain at harvest-time.

Pulp

Chardonnay ripens easily and quickly, giving plenty of juice that can be high in sugar (depending on climatic conditions). This gives good alcohol levels in the final wine. Alcohol is balanced by acids – these will fall if the grape is not picked at the critical time.

Bunch (*see* page 6)

Chardonnay is a vigorous
variety that ripens well and
can give high yields of grapes.
This is good if volume is the
aim, but top wine producers
aim for quality and intensity
of fruit character. Winemakers
restrict the enthusiasm of the
vine with strict vineyard
management by controlling
planting density and growth.

Leaf

Chardonnay's sheer
enthusiasm means that unless
wine-growers prune the vine's
leaves throughout the year
these leaves can take over
and the plant will put more
effort into making a lovely
green canopy rather than
concentrating its efforts
into ripening the grapes.

If you are lucky enough to own a piece of land in a winemaking country, you might be tempted to plant some Chardonnay. My brother-in-law has a fruit-bearing vine in his back garden — and he lives in Cambridge, England.

where chardonnay lives & why

While other grape varieties are sensitive little souls who only perform when they have a specific type of soil and certain type of climate, Chardonnay can grow anywhere happily. This is one of the reasons why it is the world's most popular quality white grape. There's little doubt that Chardonnay grown on chalk or limestone soils will produce a potentially great wine – the vineyards of Chablis, Burgundy, and Champagne have proved that. But the poor dirt of Australia and the cooler hillside sites of California are giving equally great wines, as are the irrigated plains of the Central Valley and the Riverina. The Languedoc and Central Europe give another style, as here quantity is just as important as quality. In conditions where other varieties just couldn't deliver, Chardonnay does – this grape wants to please. Plant it; give it water and it will give you masses of sweet grapes; show it some oak and it will leap straight in. What winemaker could resist?

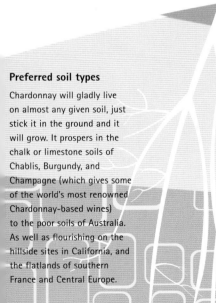

Preferred soil types

Chardonnay will gladly live
on almost any given soil, just
stick it in the ground and it
will grow. It prospers in the
chalk or limestone soils of
Chablis, Burgundy, and
Champagne (which gives some
of the world's most renowned
Chardonnay-based wines)
to the poor soils of Australia.
As well as flourishing on the
hillside sites in California, and
the flatlands of southern
France and Central Europe.

Chardonnay isn't just amenable in the vineyard, it is malleable in the winery. This is a winemaker's grape. If you want it clean and appley then ferment it at a low temperature in stainless steel tanks. If your aim is to transform your Chardonnay grapes into a complex, world-class wine then you can ferment it in barrel.

chardonnay in
good hands

Ahh... oak. Chardonnay loves oak. It can like it too much. The first oak-aged Australian and Californian Chardonnays that arrived in the UK were alcoholic, bright-yellow, and smelt of melted butter, toast, and bananas. These weren't wines you drank, they were wines you supped with a spoon. These days the same winemakers will use various techniques to curb Chardonnay's over-enthusiastic love of wood. Unoaked styles are gaining in popularity. But oak gives an extra layer of complexity to the wine – and people often expect oaky flavours. If you are making a cheap example then you can throw in bags of oak chips. Top wines will be fermented in barrel, meaning they will be less "oaky" than a wine just aged in oak, but will have extra richness and complexity. Winemakers can pick and choose techniques, Chardonnay will go along with it.

Chardonnay may well have first appeared in the Middle East. Serge Hochar, who owns Chateau Musar in Lebanon, claims that his country's best white grape, Obaideh, is in fact Chardonnay. Certainly his white wine has remarkable similarities to old-style white burgundy.

how chardonnay grew up

However, most people feel that Chardonnay first appeared in the region that has become its spiritual home, Burgundy. The fact that there is a village called Chardonnay in the Mâconnais is often given as the

clinching evidence for this, but I think all the proof you
need is to pick up a glass of great white burgundy or talk
to one of the region's winemakers. Even if Chardonnay
was born in the Lebanon this is where the techniques
for raising it to great heights were perfected.

The fascinating thing about French (and other European)
wine is the manner in which each region has maintained
its own unique character. Grapes that performed well
in one part of the country weren't, by and large, tried
elsewhere. Chardonnay is a case in point. Until relatively
recently – the 1980s in fact – it was grown primarily in
three regions, Burgundy, Chablis, and Champagne. This
has been to the benefit of winemakers and consumers, as
these three effectively have been Chardonnay laboratories
for thousands of years.

Chardonnay finally broke out of its central and northern French stronghold in the 1980s. OK, there had been plantings in other parts of the world before that, but this was when Chardonnay stopped being an anonymous grape hiding behind various appellation names and started to become what it is today – a brand.

what will become
of chardonnay?

Why did this happen? For the simple reason that people's tastes were changing. Consumers wanted wines that had fruit, wines that tasted of something but at the same time weren't too challenging. They also, suddenly, wanted a lot of wine. When it came to picking a white variety to fit all those criteria there was only one contender – Chardonnay. It's also no coincidence that its rise mirrored the global development of new winemaking technology. You want to make clean, flavoursome, yet high-volume white? Plant Chardonnay. You want to be seen as a serious, world-class winemaker? Plant Chardonnay.

Plantings continue to spread across Europe, but it has been the New World that has made Chardonnay the grape it is today. It is Australia's biggest single variety, California's main white grape, and has given Chilean, South African and Argentinean whites some much needed credibility. Its roots may be in Burgundy, but Chardonnay's destiny lies in the New World.

Chardonnay is a brand. It has become shorthand for a certain type of inoffensive white wine and is so widely planted that it's difficult to find wines that aren't Chardonnay-based on the shop shelves. This, inevitably, has led to a backlash and here lies Chardonnay's challenge. The irony is that its very versatility could be its undoing. Winemakers must start to see it less as a bland high-yielding commodity and more as a grape which, when handled with subtlety, can make truly great wines. Its challenge will be whether it can survive the growing ABC (Anything But Chardonnay) bandwagon.

the countries

Chardonnay loves to travel. Take it to sunny California
or a cool hillside in northern Italy – it will be happy
come rain or shine. So pack your bags and follow
in Chardonnay's footsteps around the world.
Its sheer variety will bowl you over.

CRIOTS-BATARD
MONTRACHET
GRAND CRU

Roger BELLAND

A SANTENAY

Chardonnay's spiritual home is France. Here you will find it in all its glorious complexity, with a huge variety of wines showing lemon zippiness to toasty, honeysuckle aromas. And the classic example is Chablis – the steely heart of Chardonnay.

france

The Chablis hierarchy

Petit (*i.e.* lesser) Chablis

Chablis Premier Cru: there are forty sites of varying quality

Chablis Grand Cru:
Blanchots
Bougros
Grenouilles
Le Clos
Preuses
Valmur
Vaudésir

Chablis – locating the taste

That glass of young Grand (or Premier) Cru Chablis has a green glint to it, a steely acidity that runs through your palate. The wine is bone-dry, yet at the centre there's a hint of roundness suggesting if you hide it away for a decade, it will open out. It tastes "flinty", "mineral". Whatever term you use, a classic Chablis isn't soft and easy-drinking. Why? Think of the location. Though the

region basks in warm, even hot, summers, winters are long, hard, and prone to frosts – and Chardonnay hates frost as much as it loves oak. To make matters more interesting, the top (Premier and Grand Cru) vineyards are planted on south-facing slopes in the narrow valley of the River Serein. They might as well invite the frost to attack. It's no surprise that many frost-limiting devices are employed to ensure Chablis' survival.

The reason the vines are planted in such a risky spot is the soil. The low- and mid-slopes of the small hills around the town of Chablis consist of a band of limestone/clay soil (aka Kimmeridgian clay) and the top sites lie on this.

Chablis has always been about purity of fruit, of allowing the vineyard, and not the winery, to show itself in the wine. This has meant that oak has been a no-no. Of course, for thousands of years winemakers would have had nothing but oak to ferment and store their wine, but

Top producers

Chablis: J.-M. Brocard
La Chablisienne co-op
G. Collet
R. Dauvissat
J. Durup
W. Fèvre
Laroche
L. Michel
L. Pinson
V. et R. Raveneau

they would have used old, neutral casks not active new ones. Things are changing. Some producers use modern technology and stainless steel fermenters to give the purest expression of Chablis, others will age for a short time in oak, but rarely exclusively new oak. That said, these days there are some who are using barrel fermentation and even malolactic fermentation to soften the wines down, but if I want a Burgundian style of wine I'll buy a burgundy. Chablis is Chardonnay's steely heart.

Burgundy

There's a pale wine in your glass. It has light aromas of lemon and apple but it tastes taut, as if there's something in its make-up that is being held back. Come back in five years, it says. You do. It has changed. Now there's nuts, honeysuckle, soft summer fruits, butter and honey and wholemeal toast. This isn't Chardonnay, this is Burgundy.

A Burgundian winemaker once told me: "I don't make Chardonnay, I make Corton-Charlemagne". That isn't Gallic pomposity – what Burgundian winemakers want to capture in their wines is the character that comes from the way the vine reacts to the soil, the sun, the altitude, the weather, and, finally, man. It's called terroir. It seems absurd until you taste wines from three adjacent sites and realise that they are totally different. The winemaking is the same, the difference is the variations in the soils, the tilt of the hill, the way the summer sun hits the vine.

Burgundy's terroir has been obsessively picked over, thanks partly to the fact that its vineyards have been endlessly subdivided over the years so that growers can have a few rows of vines in a host of different appellations. This has allowed producers to see those subtle variations between the mass of tiny sites on the south-facing limestone scarp of the Côte de Beaune. Here you find tight, mineral wines from Corton-Charlemagne, expansive buttery Meursaults which are the template for every top New World Chardonnay, the toasty structured wines from Puligny-Montrachet, and the aromatic, nuttiness of its neighbour Chassagne-Montrachet. At the pinnacle of it is Le Montrachet, a 7.5ha vineyard whose wines are the most complex whites in the world.

Knowing your Meursault from your Corton is one thing, but which of the many producers is the best? Which vintage should you go for? Burgundy frustrates as much as it excites. Find a reputable wine merchant and start tasting. It's the only way. And if you can't afford top white burgundy, but want an idea of the experience, look for wines from Rully or Montagny.

In France, Chardonnay used to be a speciality of Burgundy, Chablis, and Champagne. No longer. The tide has swept south as the variety continues its global takeover, but before we head to the Midi, it's worth looking at some of the other, longer-established Chardonnay sites.

Strictly speaking, the Mâconnais is part of southern Burgundy and chances are for most of us our first taste of a white burgundy will be one of the wines from here – probably a Pouilly-Fuissé or St-Véran. The former is, I think,

The AC system

The *appellation contrôlée* (AC) system defines the top category of French wines according to their origin. Wines from a particular appellation (defined on the bottle) are made according to regulations that specify vineyard yields, grape varieties, and production methods. Although officially the top-category AC wines are not guaranteed to be the greatest, and some disappointments are inevitable. *Vin de pays* ("country wines") are also regulated, although less strictly than AC wines. They do offer a geographical definition (eg. Vin de Pays d'Oc) and are often labelled by the grape variety. These can be more exciting, modern wines.

over-rated, the latter is Beaujolais *blanc* with a posh name. Go for a good old Mâcon *blanc* or one of the villages which add their name to the region such as Viré, Lugny, or Clessé.

Chardonnay is also grown in the eastern region of Jura where it makes a peculiarly nutty wine usually blended with the local Savagnin. The alpine region of Savoie has it too, and makes wines (often blended with Roussette and Jacquère) that are as clean and fresh as the mountain air. We're unlikely to see many of those last wines. Our experience of non-Burgundian Chardonnay will come from the Languedoc. Here the style is in line with the fat, pear and melon flavours you get from basic New World brands, not surprisingly as many of the wines are made either by Australian firms or large French firms – like the enterprising Skalli – that have realized that France can make decent, fruit-filled, varietally labelled wines. Unfortunately, many producers failed to appreciate that these days the only way to differentiate between internationally flavoured Chardonnays is by price. The fact it comes from France isn't important at this end of the market. The result has been a glut. The other option is to go for quality, which is happening in the high vineyards of Pic-St-Loup and Limoux whose barrel-fermented Chardonnays ooze class – and are much better value than lesser white burgundies.

Champagne

You must wonder quite why the first winemakers in the Champagne region decided to plant vines. This is a cool –

Top producers cont.

Languedoc: La Baume
James Herrick
Mas de Duamas Gassac

Limoux: Sieur d'Arques
Toques et Clochers (the label of an annual auction of single-barrel Chardonnays from Limoux)

Pic-St-Loup: L'Hortus

Jura: Labet
Puffeney
Tissot
Voitier

no make that cold – northerly region where grapes never achieve full ripeness but sit there tart and painfully acidic. This does not make modern, sun-filled wine bursting with fat tropical fruits, but if the aim is to make a high-class sparkling wine then that acidity isn't a hindrance, it is a positive asset. The chalk soil is ideal for producing a white wine with delicacy and finesse. And the ever-obliging Chardonnay fits the bill. The bulk of these plantings are on the eastern slopes of the Côte des Blancs south of Epernay, with the best wines coming from Cramant, Ogier, Mesnil, and Vertrus, all of which produce a fragrant, elegant style. Chardonnay in the Montagne de Reims is zippier while that from the Côtes de Sézanne in the south is richer.

You will rarely come across single-vineyard Champagne – and when you do you'll pay a high price. The art of making this wine lies in blending, not just different vineyards, but different varieties: Chardonnay, Pinot Noir and Pinot Meunier. Blending is important not just because it allows houses to produce large volumes, but it allows winemakers to produce a more complex wine than they would have been able to get from one site. Chardonnay in Champagne has quality but it doesn't have the multifaceted complexity of burgundy. To discover what the variety brings to Champagne try a *Blanc de Blancs* Champagne which is made exclusively from Chardonnay, or the rare but softly sublime Crémant de Cramant. You can still easily discern the Chardonnay element in any good Champagne though. Do you detect a lemony lift, the aromas of elderflower, the creamy softness, and maybe some light nuttiness? That's Chardonnay doing its work.

Chardonnay plantings are on the rise in Italy, particularly in the south, where it is still mostly used as a blender. Yet as Italian winemakers strive to achieve their own style of cool, restrained elegance, there may be a few surprises in store.

italy

Top producers

Piemonte: Gaja
Icardi
Moccagata
Sinaglio

Franciacorta:
Bellavista Castaldi
Cà del Bosco

Alto Adige: Dorigo
Cantina S. Michele
Appiano
Villa Russiz
Tiefenbruner

Winemakers in the northeastern region of Piemonte have embraced the variety, which seems only appropriate since the great red grape of the region, Nebbiolo, has similarities with Pinot Noir: superb at its best, dreadful otherwise. Piemonte's cool hills and low yields are giving high-quality Chardonnay – at high prices. Why does burgundy spring to mind again?

In Lombardy the variety is used predominantly for sparkling wines, the most elegant of which come from

Franciacorta. Some producers, most notably Cà del Bosco, are also making superb barrel-fermented still wines. The two areas most likely to challenge Piemonte are Friuli and Alto Adige, where more restrained, top-end examples are appearing. The real surprise for many people is the fact that one of Italy's top Chardonnays comes not from the cool north but from Sicily. Planeta's magnificent wine also demonstrates the current battle between market and winemaker – he wants a more restrained style, but the market demands big and oaky. It's Italy's dilemma and it's almost as if the country is going through the same evolution that happened in Australia a decade ago. At the other end of the market, high-yielding bland Chardonnay is being used to bulk out anonymous blends. Things are improving though. A better grasp of barrel and vineyard is giving well-balanced wines, while top producers are making classy unoaked examples – or blending together oaked and unoaked wines. That shows understanding.

Top producers cont

Friuli: Collavini
Marco Felluga
Jermann
Vie de Romans

Tuscany: Antinori
Isole e Olena

Sicily: Planeta
Tasca d'Almerita

The DOC system

In Italy, DOC wines are those of controlled origin, from specific regions, made with specified grape varieties and to regulated styles – it's the equivalent of French AC (see page 23). DOCG indicates even stricter controls, but neither DOC nor DOCG guarantee top quality. IGT is the equivalent of *vin de pays*.

When you consider what has happened in the rest of the world, Chardonnay has made relatively little impact on Spain. But the Spanish are finding new ways to develop its potential.

spain

Top producers

Penèdes: Augustus
Jean León
Torres

Allela: Marques de
Allela

Navarra: Chivite
Monjardin

La Mancha: Manuel
Mananeque

Spain has relatively few quality white varieties – Verdejo, Albariño, and Godello are regional specialities. This is red wine drinking country – if people want white they drink pink. The best Chardonnays come from an arc running (roughly) from Barcelona to Bilbao. Spain is hot and if you are wanting character in your Chardonnay that means seeking out cool sites.

That's what has happened in Catalonia, which has always made wines that seem to look across the border to France, rather than into central Spain. The hillside sites give good, if relatively short-lived, Chardonnays, such as Augustus and Torres' single-vineyard, Milmanda. The tiny DO of Allela also makes a good example, especially since they have toned down the oak. After a considerable battle, Chardonnay is also permitted to be used in *cava* where it gives finesse and some roundness to the wines.

The benefit of lower temperatures is shown in the decent Chardonnays from the high lands of Somontano, but even greater potential has been shown in the wines from cool northern Navarra. Here Monjardin makes an excellent Chardonnay that won't break the bank, but their wine is overshadowed by what I believe to be Spain's greatest example of the grape – that from Chivite. The firm, bravely, decided not to put Chardonnay on the label but instead let people assess the wine on its own term. A brave decision – but one that has paid off. Unusually for a serious non-burgundian Chardonnay it is restrained, elegant, and capable of medium-term ageing.

The benefits of cool or relatively cool sites hasn't stopped Chardonay being planted across the rest of the country, where, not surprisingly, it makes pretty bland, uninteresting wines that manage to hit a desireable price point and give some spurious credibility to a blend. One exception is the Manuel Mananeque Chardonnay from La Mancha though its quality is partly down to the fact that the vineyard is at 1,000 metres (3,280 feet)!

The northwest of the country may well yet prove to be one of the most exciting areas for the variety. On paper, the Galician DOs of Ribeira Sacra and Ribeiro would seem to have possibilities though they may prove to be too wet.

A better bet is the inland region of Valdeorras (home to the wonderful Godello variety). Time will tell whether Chardonnay is about to make another great conquest.

The DO system

In Spain, DO wines are those of controlled origin, from specific regions, made with specified grape varieties and to regulated styles – it's the equivalent of French AC (*see* page 23). DOCa indicates even stricter controls, but neither DO nor DOCa guarantee top quality. *Crianza*, *Reserva*, and *Gran Reserva* indicate oak ageing.

No winemaking country has escaped the globalisation of Chardonnay. That said, it has not yet attained the status of number one white grape throughout Europe the way it has in the Americas and Australia.

central & eastern europe

This is mostly due to tradition and also because there are already plenty of native white grape varieties that do the same job very effectively. Portugal and Austria are both good cases in point. There are Portuguese Chardonnays, some extremely good ones – particularly from the south – but the country has such a wealth of indigenous grapes that when the winemaking revolution hit, it made more sense to improve what was already in the ground than bring in something new. Austria is much the same. Chardonnay has been grown in small quantities for centuries, but even though plantings are growing, Austria's winemakers have concentrated on Grüner Veltliner and

Weissburgunder... and recently Sauvignon Blanc. There are good Chardonnays though, the feature of which is a naturally high acidity. Get that in balance and tone down the over-enthusiastic oaking and some truly great wines will appear. Greece, too, has turned to the vines already in the ground and Chardonnay has yet to make a big impact. Look to the limestone soils of Nemea for the best.

The situation is totally different in Eastern Europe. The 1980s wine boom was partly fuelled by Chardonnay from Bulgaria. It was clean, well-made white (and cheap), but the next step up in quality has never come. Confused privatization, messy land deals, and a general lack of investment has meant Bulgaria still manages to make straightforward white wine that happens to be Chardonnay. Hungary was touted briefly as having greater potential but has yet to deliver. Romania and Moldova were each seen as the new Bulgaria at one stage, but both are in an even worse state. Lack of investment in both, plus the attentions of the Russian mafia in the latter, have put paid to early expectations. It's hard to see Eastern Europe as being anything other than a source of cheap fruit.

Top producers

(Some of Eastern Europe's more attractive whites appear under own-labels in UK supermarkets. These wines can be great value for money.)

Austria: Lenz Moser
F.X. Pichler
Polz
Sattler
Stiegelmar (Juris)
Tement

Greece: Antonopoulos
Boutari
Domaine Hatzimichali
Papaïoannou

Strange to think that thirty years ago Chardonnay was virtually unknown in Australia. Today it is the country's most widely planted grape. While there is no doubt that soft, toasty, often buttery, peachy Chardonnay helped the phenomenal growth of Aussie wines in the 1980s and 1990s, the variety is now standing at the crossroads.

australia

The rich, yellow-hued butterscotch styles of the past have gone and winemakers are looking for elegant, long-lived wines that reflect their place of origin rather than the barrel they were aged in. Yes, Oz has discovered terroir.

New South Wales

Lower Hunter Valley Chardonnay was probably the first Aussie white most of us tasted, though the region was first planted not for its ideal conditions but because it was near Sydney and is now handy for wine tourists. Still, with a good site some rich, honeyed Chardonnay can be made.

The Upper Hunter is better suited, giving big fruit flavours and a buttery texture. Rosemount's Roxburgh, whose oak has been toned down significantly, is the classic example. Cowra makes soft, rich wines, as does Mudgee, but for great NSW Chardonnay head high to Orange where the cool climate produces intense, limey/tangerine-flavoured wines.

South Australia

Barossa Valley Chardonnay does exist, but it tends to be big and fat. McLaren Vale has big-boned, succulent examples, but the top region is the Adelaide Hills where the best examples are reaching new levels of refinement.

The Hills are peopled by stubborn perfectionists who produce great barrel-fermented Chardonnays that show pure fruit, finesse, and a clean elegance. Those big Chardonnays that filled the mouth when one year old

Top producers

New South Wales:
Canobolas
Cowra
Mudgee
Rosemount
Scarborough
Tyrell
VAT 47

South Australia:
Chain of Ponds
Geoff Weaver
Grosset
M3
Petaluma
Shaw & Smith
Yattarna

and collapsed in a heap three years later are now on the way out, but to be safe trust the producer – the region is just an indicator.

South East Australia

If you want to find the vineyards that took Australia from curiosity to the UK's favourite wine-producing country then follow the Murray and Murrumbidgee rivers. Here are the big, irrigated plantings sprawling into Victoria, New South Wales, and South Australia and the source of all the South East Australian Chardonnay we still gleefully glug. Heat + water + vines + huge tanks + bags of oak chips = bottled sunshine, aka soft, undemanding Chardonnay that tastes of tropical fruits. Not exciting, boring in fact, but bloody reliable.

Victoria

The high-quality side of Victorian Chardonnay is to be found in the Yarra Valley. Not only is this cool region home to many of Australia's top sparkling winemakers, but it produces clean, citric, and fine-bodied Chardonnays. A cool seaside climate is the key to the crisp wines from Mornington Peninsula and Geelong.

Margaret River

The best of Margaret River's elegant, barrel-fermented Chardonnays have richness of fruit, superb concentration, and age well. Again, though, be guided by the producer, not the region.

Tasmania

The same is true of Tasmania. The coolest of the island
state's sites gives super-clean, lemony fruit for fine-boned
sparkling wines while a few are leading the way with
intense still wines.

These days, Australian Chardonnay lies in three distinct
groupings. Melon and tinned pears at the bottom end;
a broad band of decent, but Identikit wines in the
middle and a small grouping of exceptional wines
at the top. This last group – where winemakers
have taken the foot off the gas and allowed
the vineyard to speak – is the future.

There aren't many countries these days where Chardonnay is overshadowed by another variety, but New Zealand has always done its own thing. So, while the country's Sauvignon Blanc is hyped-up, Kiwi Chardonnay is, if anything, underrated.

new zealand

Top producers

Hawke's Bay: Delegat's
Esk Valley
Morton Estate
Sileni

Martinborough:
Martinbourough Vineyards
Palliser Estate

Central Otago: Felton Road
Giesen

Marlborough: Cloudy Bay
Hunters
Isabel Estate

The word intense is often overused when talking of New Zealand whites but it is accurate. While Sauvignon Blanc can be almost too piercingly clean, the best Chardonnays marry that clean, pure fruit and crisp acidity with often surprising weight. The grape is grown throughout the country, but there are real character differences between the best regions.

The bulk of the major commercial plantings are in Gisborne and the wines made are sound, solid and reliable. Fans of a fleshy, tropical fruit style (think mangoes and peaches) should seek out wines from Hawkes Bay – there are some good examples of this broad, quite relaxed kind of wine, though it can get a bit floppy. The problem in New Zealand for once isn't wood, it's achieving a balance between ripe fruit and acidity.

The opposite style can be found in the southern tip of both North and South Islands, specifically in Martinborough and Central Otago, which isn't that surprising since they also produce the country's best Pinot Noir. Both regions make clean, intense (it's that word again!), citric Chardonnays that will age well. The best Chardonnays, however, come from what's considered Sauvignon Blanc territory, Marlborough. Here the best producers manage to meld the rich fruit of Hawke's Bay with the citrus and structure from Martinborough into a complete, complex, balanced package.

Sauvingon Blanc may continue to capture people's attention but the quality of Kiwi Chardonnay is growing with each vintage. A country and a style to watch closely.

America just luurves Chardonnay. Yet this is where the ABC (Anything But Chardonnay) club was founded – by winemakers, writers, and restaurateurs who were sick of the variety. Their efforts have produced some great wines, but have made little impact on Chardonnay's grip on the nation's consciousness.

north america

North California

The heart of top-end Californian Chardonnay lies many miles to the north in the affluent Napa and Sonoma Valleys. This is where the classic Californian style was first crafted. Super-ripe grapes, American oak barrels, and high levels of alcohol, gave huge wines that were unlike anything that had ever come out of Europe and which appealed to a country that believes that big is beautiful.

California's Chardonnays are, by and large, still big wines, but a new restraint has emerged in recent years. Rather than aging in vanilla-heavy American oak barrels, top producers began to ferment in French oak and started to look for cooler sites. In the Napa this meant uprooting all the Chardonnay in the hot centre and (hotter) north and replanting in the cooler area of Carneros or moving to the hills. In Sonoma it meant seeking out the little valleys that were exposed to the sea like the Russian and Alexander Valleys, both of which, like Carneros, are good for still and sparkling wines, but the top-end wines are still pricey. The most surprising evidence of Sonoma's quality came when Gallo, the king of bulk-wine production, remodelled a tract of land into a purpose-built vineyard and produced some classy wines.

In the far north is the centre of the state's organic movement where you'll find some good, impressively fleshy wines. There are also some notable new, high-

Top producers

North California: Beringer
Carneros Creek
Château Potelle
Clos de Bois
Kistler
Phelps
Saintsbury
Simi

altitude vineyards near the coast that are showing that there are even more parts of the state as yet untapped.

South California

America's very welcome discovery of wine has led to massive plantings in the Central Valley, much of it Chardonnay, and it is this area, along with a revived Monterey, that are the source for most of the new mid-priced wines we see here in the UK. The Californian wine industry has always been consumer driven and ever since these new large vineyards have started splurging forth fruit it has realised it needs somewhere to sell it. Since the domestic market isn't growing as rapidly as anticipated that means export – and in particular that means targeting the UK. For once the Californian industry is making mid-market wines that are better suited to the UK palate (lower in alcohol, less sweet than the American drinkers like, even unoaked), and at prices that are more in tune with our pockets.

The regions in the south of the state don't just produce large volumes of decent-value Chardonnay, they are home to its greatest and most elegant examples. To find them you have to seek out the limestone soils of Mount Harlan and the cooler regions near to Santa Barbara, in particular the Edna and Santa Ynez Valleys. A cool climate but strong sun means ripeness and acidity. And, you suspect, a location far away from the glitz of LA or San Francisco allows winemakers to get on with making great wines. Expect to pay Burgundian prices, but expect a similar level of quality.

Top producers cont.

South California:
Au Bon Climat
Chalone

The rest of North America

When west-coast winemakers of a certain generation decided to do things their own way, they headed to the Pacific Northwest, and settled in the cool Willamette Valley in Oregon. They planted first Pinot Noir and then Chardonnay, figuring that the climate was similar to that of Burgundy. The industry thought they were mad, but the hunch paid off. Though there were wild variations between vintages in the early years, the right vines are now in the right sites and plantings are growing, most recently into the Dundee Hills. At its best Oregon Chardonnay is superbly well-balanced and elegant.

Across the border in Washington State the situation is a little different. Here the majority of the vineyards are on the other side of the Cascade Mountain range, stuck in the high, dry desert of the Yakima Valley. Nothing would grow here were it not for the irrigation provided by the huge Columbia River. Wineries tend to be bigger than the boutiques of Oregon and the style more consumer-friendly (and well-priced), especially to UK drinkers.

It is claimed that wine is made in every other state. As far as Chardonnay is concerned the best are from Long Island and the Finger Lakes in New York State – harder to find, but extremely good wines with clean fruit flavours, and evidence that the west doesn't have it all its own way. There are plantings in Texas that have been talked up, Texan-style, for years, but have yet to deliver. Better turn to Canada – either Ontario for rich wines or the Okanagan Valley in British Columbia for a crisper style.

South America's Chardonnays are well-priced and well-made, packed with juicy fruit, with a hint of oak and clean acidity. The problem is sameness of style. Can they break out of the mid-market and make the next step up to top producer?

south america

Chile

For me, Chile makes the most reliable medium-priced Chardonnays in the world at the moment. The industry is evolving rapidly. Investment is increasing, the number of wineries is growing and quality is amazingly consistent. As far as Chardonnay is concerned, the region to watch remains Casablanca which, though it can be prone to late-spring frosts just after the tender buds have formed, (like in Chablis) is making the best balanced wines with

good rich fruits and clean acidity. All well and good. The one problem with Chile is a sameness of style. Things are beginning to change as winemakers get a better handle on their vineyards. Until they do, Chile will remain Mr Reliable at a certain price but not, sadly, Mr Remarkable.

Argentina

It was only recently that Argentinean wine was poised to explode onto the UK market. Then the country's economy imploded and the international investment that had been pouring in dried up. One region was seen as having the best potential for Chardonnay. At an altitude of over 1,200 metres (3,936 feet), Tupungato lies in the foothills of the Andes and the combination of height, cool breezes, and intense sunlight gives wines with great fruit and, importantly, clean fresh acidity. When the economic situation clears up, this will offer the top-end Chardonnnays that will prove this country's vast potential.

Top producers

Chile: Casablanca
Errázuriz
Villard

Argentina: Catena
Finca Flichman

Argentina has huge potential, but South Africa is currently the most exciting wine-producing country in the world. The progress which has been made in the few short years since apartheid ended has been quite phenomenal.

south africa

With it has come a dismantling of a bureaucratic system that stifled creativity, the emergence of small, quality-oriented estates, and a young generation of well-travelled winemakers. The vineyards have been re-assessed and extensively replanted, with the most appropriate varieties now being planted in the best-suited sites. The transformation is total and the results hugely impressive.

The bulk of the standard South African Chardonnay hails either from plantings in Worcester or the huge grape farms situated along the Olifants River. The scale of the operations here are mind-blowing – there is one tank in a winery in Vredendal that holds as much as New Zealand's entire crop.

The wines are standard, international styles – solid, slightly off-dry, with peach and tinned pear fruits. If you are searching for something of a higher standard then you could do worse than go to the region that first showed the potential Chardonnay had in the country, Robertson. This, too, is a bulk-oriented region and was widely dismissed by the quality-driven winemakers over the mountains in Paarl,

Franschhoek, and Stellenbosch. Yet it was here that a winemaker called Danie de Wet showed the South African wine industry that quality Chardonnay could be made. His range now includes single vineyard, unwooded, and barrel-fermented examples.

Chardonnay is planted in every region, and while you will find a few richly flavoured, big-boned examples from the hot region of Paarl, the top examples at the moment are coming from the hillsides in Franschhoek, and a variety of sites in Stellenbosch. But it would be wrong to believe that there is a single style from the two latter regions. The consumer can choose from old-style, New World, rich-yellow, buttery examples, to wines where the oak is toned down but the richness of fruit is still in evidence. There is also a newer wave of Chardonnays where restraint is the key and a balance has been struck between zesty, limey, mealy fruit, and a subtle creamy texture. There are barrel-aged and barrel-fermented wines, as well as unoaked ones.

Elegant Chardonnays are coming from Walker Bay, which, after all, is where South Africa's top Pinot Noirs hail from. Bouchard-Finlayson and Hamilton Russell both make beautifully balanced, elegant wines that have that elusive "mineral" note that is rarely found outside Burgundy. That's far from the end of the story. This is a new South Africa and untapped sites are constantly being explored. The fruit-growing area of Elgin is one that is showing potential and, as one winemaker pointed out to me, the best wine-growing regions may not even have been planted yet. Exciting times.

Top producers

L'Avenir
Avontuur
Bouchard-Finlayson
Danie de Wet
Delaire
Eikendal
Glen Carlou
Hamilton Russell
Jordan
Longrdige
Louisvale
Meerlust
Neil Ellis
Rustenberg
Springfield
Thelema
Vergelegen

There's Chardonnay sprinkled across most of the rest of the world – clean light wines from Slovenia and Slovakia, ethereal precise ones from Switzerland — even China has started to get in on the act. Let's start off a little closer to home.

the rest of the world

Top producers

UK: Nyetimber

Israel: Carmel
Gamla
Yarden

Lebanon: Kefraya
Chateau Musar

As I write this I am looking out at a chalk downland. I'm in a climate that is pleasant enough, but it's cool and doesn't always allow fruit to ripen. Where have you heard that before? That's right, Champagne. I'm not saying that the conditions in Sussex are identical to those in northern France, but it does give a hint as to what style of wine English producers should be concentrating on – sparkling. Nyetimber has shown the way forward and more are set to follow. Chardonnay is making another conquest.

It has also made a landfall in Israel which, since the founding of Golan Heights winery, has been making increasingly good, modern fruit-filled wines – though prices are a bit steep. In recent years smaller wineries such as Dalton have raised the stakes further. Once again, the wines are made in a toasty Californian mould. If Israel looks to America, then Lebanon looks to old-style France. Obaideh and Merweh are ultra-traditional heavy white wines, but the old vintages have a wonderful charm and, since Obaideh could be the original Chardonnay, this is more or less where we started.

MIS EN BOUTEILLES A LA PROPRIÉTÉ

PRODUCE OF

Meur

"Le Limo

APPELLATION MEURS

...5% vol   Alain COCHE

Propriétaire-Récoltant à Meur

buying, storing, & serving

Now you know about the variations and you're ready to seek out some classy Chardonnay. You know what a hard-working grape it is, so let's treat it with respect. Here are some tips on on how to select it, store it, and serve it. Plus some other white wines to try.

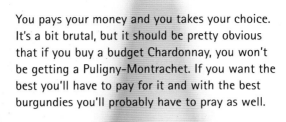

You pays your money and you takes your choice. It's a bit brutal, but it should be pretty obvious that if you buy a budget Chardonnay, you won't be getting a Puligny-Montrachet. If you want the best you'll have to pay for it and with the best burgundies you'll probably have to pray as well.

quality vs price

Entry-level

Since Chardonnay is fast becoming the most widely planted white grape and most of those new vineyards are in warm, irrigated sites, there's going to be plenty of Chardonnay at the value-for-money end of the price spectrum. By that I mean wines that show ripe flavours, have a bit of natural sweetness, and that could have seen the addition of oak chips (see page 12). There's nothing wrong with these wines – they are perfectly well made. It's just that they lack personality. Whether they come from Chile, Hungary, Australia, or France, they will taste much the same. That's the point. These wines are mass-produced to hit a certain price point and taste a certain way. They are the same as tomatoes, or battery-farmed chickens.

Mid-market

You get a better selection and more character here. In the New World seek out the better quality, single-vineyard

Chardonnays from Chile. The well-made and poised
Robertson Chardonnays in South Africa are worth looking
at, too. In New Zealand, try Marlborough, Hawke's Bay,
and Otago. In Australia, have a look for unoaked examples
from Adelaide Hills. You can pick up "second label" wines
from regions such as the McLaren Vale, Yarra, Clare, and
Margaret River that might not have the complexity of the
top-end wines but give you an idea of the regional style.

Similarly in the USA. Try Santa Barbara, Sonoma, and
Mendocino rather than Napa. Look for excellent examples
in Washington State. In Europe, you should start looking
at Austria and the new Italian wines. In France, Chablis
is now within your sights, and the Mâconnais in Burgundy
gives softer, more honeyed wines, offering great value, as
do the "lesser" appellations St-Aubin, Rully, and Montagny.

Top-end
You have the money? Then get thee to Burgundy – or
at least to a wine merchant who specializes in burgundy.
Knowing that the greatest white wines in the world come
from Puligny- and Chassagne-Montrachet is one thing,
knowing which producer to choose is the trick. Your guide
appointed, you can then compare them with Meursault,
with Corton-Charlemagne, or a Chablis Grand Cru. *Then*
you can see what winemakers the world over are trying to
emulate. Of the rest, in Italy poke around in Piemonte, in
the USA try Carneros, Napa, Sonoma but most of all Santa
Barbara, and, in good years, Oregon. In Australia three
regions stand out: Margaret River, Clare, and Yarra.

You mean there are other white grapes? By the look of the wine shelves it would be easy to believe that Chardonnay is the only white grape in the world and, while it is possible to stay within the Chardonnay camp and drink everything from fizzy to unwooded to oaked, it is worth exploring alternatives. For those of you who like the crisp unwooded style there are a huge number of grape varieties that will tickle your fancy. Sauvignon Blanc from the Loire (Sancerre, Pouilly-Fumé, Menetou-Salon, Quincy) has a clean, zesty gooseberry character while examples from New Zealand are wonderfully intense – as are the best from the Constantia region of South Africa and the Sauvignon/Verdejo blends from Rueda in Spain.

other wines to try

If you are browsing the Spanish section keep an eye out for Albariño from Galicia. With soft pulpy fruit (apricot, ripe pear, peach) and fresh acidity it is a great food wine.

It would also be worth exploring the outer reaches of Italian white wine such as some of the magnificent top-end Soaves. Those made by producers such as Pieropon, Anselmi, and Ca' Rugate in both oaked and unoaked styles are filled with the aromas of cut flowers and fresh pear. Gavi (made from Cortese) has aromas of nut and citrus fruits and is another great food wine, as is the intense mix of almond and peach from Piemonte's Arneis.

Though fresh Italian Pinot Grigio appears to be enjoying a renaissance I think the best examples of this variety come from Alsace where they are honeyed but fresh, or Oregon where they are fleshy, silky, rounded, and great with seafood. Ideal for people who don't want too much oak. Nor can you ignore the truly magnificent wines from Riesling in Germany and Alsace. Think crisp apples, flowers, and a hint of honey. Delicious and refreshing.

Oak fans should look to Sémillon and, though this seems perverse, to mature (eight years plus) un-oaked Semillon (no é) from Australia's Hunter Valley. Why? Because the variety picks up unbelievable aromas of toast and lime even though it has never seen the inside of a barrel. I'd also have a look at the superbly elegant Sémillon/Sauvignon blends form Bordeaux (Graves especially) and Australia's Margaret River. These are wines that will age beautifully.

We live in an instant world and the result is that most wines these days are produced to be consumed as soon as they are bought or at least within a couple of days or so. Most of us don't have the cellar (or the patience) required to store bottles for lengthy periods of time. This means that the majority of the Chardonnays that you'll come across in your trawls up and down the wine shelves are pick-me-up and drink-me-right-now wines.

when to serve

There are, however, some Chardonnays that not only get better with bottle-age but which need it. One of the challenges facing non-Burgundian Chardonnay makers is producing wines that develop complexity in bottle, the success of which depends on the acid structure of the wine.

Timescale for storage
Grand and Premier Cru Chablis: up to ten years.
Top white burgundies: a decade or so after the vintage.
Lesser white burgundies: happily for up to five years.
Top-end New World: best to aim for five to seven years.

The good news is that since Chardonnay has taken over the world there is a style to suit every occasion, from a party wine that you need large volumes of at a low price, to great wines you want to share with with a few friends.

For some reason we rarely treat white wine as seriously as we do red. It is often the palate cleanser at the beginning of the meal rather than the centrepiece. Needless to say Chardonnay can fulfil both requirements. Those crisp, unwooded examples from Australia, Italy, and France (Chablis especially) are the perfect wines for lunchtime and are as good on their own as they are with food. Equally, these are the best wines for drinking in the summer when their clean, zesty flavours freshen up your mouth and match light summery foods perfectly.

The converse is also true. Top-end rich, nutty, mature Chardonnays are dinner wines to be served on a grand occasion. They are full-bodied and need time to open in the glass. Wines to to be sipped over a meal rather than knocked back at a picnic.

If you have a great mature burgundy or top New World example then treat it as you would a great red wine, make it the focus of the meal.

In a glass is the obvious answer, though there are plenty of bottom-end Chardonnays on the market that would be best served in a bucket. Glassware has become quite a science in recent years with people such as Georg Riedel not just making the case but proving that the shape of the glass does affect the taste of the wine. Needless to say that means he has produced a vast range of glasses for not only each grape variety but even individual styles.

how to serve

Don't panic though, you won't need them all, but if you are serving a top-end Chardonnay do try to use a long-stemmed glass with a medium-sized bowl (slightly smaller than a red wine glass, and don't overfill the glass either, give the wine room to breathe. Champagne should always be served in flutes – though half and quarter bottles can be drunk straight from the bottle with a straw.

What temperature the wine should be served at? The fact is we tend to serve white wines far too cold. Remember that a wine is there to be tasted, savoured, enjoyed. You can't do that if it is served at the wrong temperature. What's the point of buying a good wine (and there's no excuse at this stage for *not* buying one) and obliterating its qualities by over-enthusiastic chilling?

That said, it should be served cool. A crisp, unwooded example will taste that bit fresher having spent a little time in the fridge; one with lashings of oak won't be quite so heavy.

It is dangerous being prescriptive in these matters, but Champagne served at just below 10°C (50°F) is just about right, though by the time you are pouring the third glass the wine will actually taste that little bit better.

A good everyday Chardonnay will be at its best at around 10°C (50°F) so don't serve it straight from the fridge. If you have bought a top-end white burgundy or great New World example then serve it cool, maybe at 12°C (54°F) and decant it. Yes, that's right. Treat any great white like a great red.

The key to food and wine matching is do what you think is right for you. You will not be arrested by the food and wine police for enjoying Chardonnay with steak or baked beans!

what to serve with

Serve Chardonnay with whatever you want to. Wine and food are there to be enjoyed. Here are a few tips to maximize that.

1. The key to a good match often lies with the sauce. Chardonnay works well with creamy sauces, so chicken, veal, pork, or pasta are fine if they're served in this way, but are less successful if the sauce is richer, or tomato-based. Chardonnay and roast pork or chicken are great.

2. Oak might give an extra element to Chardonnay, but there is little doubt that it can get in the way with food. Lightly oaked or unoaked Chardonnays are a safer bet than huge, heavily oaked wines, but if that is what you've got, then try a squeeze of lemon juice on that piece of fish. It will help reduce the impact of the wood.

3. Light wines go with lighter foods, so serve light/unoaked Chardonnays and clean, crisp Chablis with all seafood, cold meats, and salads (but don't use a vinegar-heavy dressing, capers, gherkins, or lots of raw onions!). Chardonnay is also surprisingly good with moderately spicy Indian food and Ken Hom maintains that white burgundy is the best bet with classic Chinese cuisine.

4. The cardinal rule is: the better the wine, the simpler the food should be. You want to ensure the wine is the star – you've paid a lot of money for it after all.

5. Champagne goes with everything.

index